This book gave me a lot of examples on how to calm my body when I am angry and frustrated. I will remember these things and use them when I feel angry. I think this book will help a lot of kids who get frustrated easily.

Jack, age 10

This book helped me know what to do when I am feeling sad or mad or scared, like go to the calming space or do my breathing.

Ezra, age 5

This book has some great tips and tricks for helping boys with their anxiety, worry, and anger. I learned a lot about how my brain works when I am anxious. Understanding this helps me know what to do when I am anxious. I would recommend this book to boys my age and younger.

Knox, age 12

I think this book will be like a flashlight to help you find your way on a dark path. I really hope this book reminds boys that God is always here to help them.

Jackson, age 10

I'm glad Mr. David wrote this book. I love baseball, but basketball makes my belly hurt and makes it hard to breathe before a game. I sometimes cry and say I don't want to play. My mom and I are filling a toolbox to help me. I put a journal in there to draw.

Ford, age 7

My feelings chart helps me see what I'm feeling, and my guitar helps me get my angry stuff out.

Judah, age 6

STRONG
AND SMART

STRONG
AND

A BOY'S GUIDE TO BUILDING HEALTHY EMOTIONS

SMART

David Thomas, LMSW

Illustrated by Heath McPherson

BETHANYHOUSE

a division of Baker Publishing Group

Minneapolis, Minnesota

Published by Bethany House Publishers
11400 Hampshire Avenue South
Minneapolis, Minnesota 55438
www.bethanyhouse.com

Bethany House Publishers is a division of
Baker Publishing Group, Grand Rapids, Michigan

Printed in the United States of America

ISBN 978-0-7642-3999-1 (paperback)
ISBN 978-1-4934-3941-6 (ebook)
Library of Congress Control Number: 2021061895

Scripture quotations are from the Holy Bible, New International Version®. NIV®. Copyright © 1973, 1978, 1984, 2011 by Biblica, Inc.™ Used by permission of Zondervan. All rights reserved worldwide. www.zondervan.com. The "NIV" and "New International Version" are trademarks registered in the United States Patent and Trademark Office by Biblica, Inc.™

Some names and recognizable details have been changed to protect the privacy of those who have shared their stories for this book.

The information in this book is intended solely as an educational resource, not a tool to be used for medical diagnosis or treatment. The information presented is in no way a substitute for consultation with a personal health care professional. Readers should consult their personal health care professional before adopting any of the suggestions in this book or drawing inferences from the text. The author and publisher specifically disclaim all responsibility for any liability, loss, or risk, personal or otherwise, which is incurred as a consequence, directly or indirectly, of the use of and/or application of any of the contents of this book.

Cover design by Dan Pitts
Interior illustrations by Heath McPherson

Baker Publishing Group publications use paper produced from sustainable forestry practices and post-consumer waste whenever possible.

23 24 25 26 27 28   7 6 5 4 3

Contents

This book is dedicated to the hundreds of strong and smart
boys I've had the honor of knowing in my work.
You are superheroes.

Hello

My name is David, and I'm a counselor who works with boys and their parents. I've been doing this work for twenty-five years. I have a yellow lab named Owen. He's like many boys I meet with—he has a lot of energy, likes to be active, and loves people.

Owen is a therapy dog, which means he went to school for a long time to learn to be helpful when kids feel big feelings. He likes to celebrate when they feel happy about their birthday, winning a soccer game, learning a new instrument, or building a Lego project. He wants to be supportive when kids feel sad about their grandparent dying, a family dog being sick, not getting picked for a team, or their parents getting a divorce. He hopes to be helpful when kids feel angry about finishing screen time, annoying siblings, hurtful friends, or losing a baseball game.

Owen is loyal and loving. He's a good listener and extremely patient. I learn a lot from him about how to be a supportive friend.

He's helped me and boys I spend time with learn how to be a better son, brother, and friend. He does have a bad habit of standing too close. He's learning to give people more personal space. Sometimes he licks folks when they don't want to be licked. He's just trying to be friendly, but sometimes people want some alone time. These are hard lessons to learn, aren't they?

Owen has helped a lot of boys learn how to work through big emotions like sad, lonely, and angry. That's an important thing to learn. This workbook is going to help you do that. If you're reading this with your parent, my guess is that you're already strong and smart, like the title of this workbook. You have good ideas. You're a great problem-solver. Your teachers would call you an awesome student.

I bet you're strong as well. You may be able to run fast, lift heavy things, and play challenging sports. I'm glad you can already do many things with your brain and body. I want to help you build strong and smart *emotional* muscles too.

Think about Superman. You know how strong he is. He can lift trains and planes. He's also really smart. He knows when people are in danger and who the bad guys are. He doesn't just have strong *physical* muscles, he has strong *emotional* muscles. He cares deeply for his friends and family. He cares about all of humanity, or he wouldn't put himself in the way of danger. That's what makes him heroic. That's the kind of strong and smart we're working toward.

Becoming emotionally strong.

When we are emotionally strong and smart, we can work through frustrating moments without yelling at people we love. We can be sad with our friends when they are hurting. We can become supportive to classmates who need a friend, because, like Superman, we can tell they are having a hard time.

Being emotionally strong and smart is like a superpower.

Being emotionally strong and smart is like a superpower. You know how Spider-Man has a Spidey sense? He can sense danger, immediately makes a plan, and springs into action.

God designed our bodies to signal us in the same way. If we learn to listen to those signals, they can be clues telling us what's happening, and we can brainstorm what to do and then spring into action.

Batman is another superhero who can do amazing things. He has a signal that tells him when he's needed. As long as he pays attention to the Bat-Signal, he can jump into the Batmobile and be ready to help. If Batman stopped paying attention to the Bat-Signal, or if Spider-Man ignored his Spidey sense, there would be more danger and less help.

The same is true for us. If we ignore the signs and signals inside of us, dangerous things can happen, like yelling and saying hurtful things, arguing and talking back, throwing things, and being disrespectful. There's an old saying that "hurt people *hurt* people." When we are hurting, it's easy to be hurtful to others unless we learn to be strong and smart. Building emotional muscles helps us stop taking the hurt out on ourselves and other people.

I know grown-ups who are hurting and who keep hurting other people because they never learned to build emotional muscles so they could be strong and smart. It makes it hard to have healthy relationships when we keep hurting people because we are hurting. So let's get strong and smart together. Let's learn to notice our Bat-Signals and pay attention to our Spidey sense. Because the world needs more superheroes who are strong and smart, tough and tender, loyal and loving.

Draw a picture of yourself as a superhero. What superpowers do you already have? What powers would you like to have?

The Builder and the Fisherman

One of my grandfathers was a builder. He fought in World War II, came home to care for his family, and learned to build houses. I went to work for him one summer, and together, with his crew, we built a home on a large piece of land.

When I was five years old, he gave me my first toolbox. It was made of wood, and he carved my name on the side. He bought me my first tools, and I would carry them around the house in my toolbox, pretending to build and fix things. Then I learned to use my tools to really build things in my room, the garage, and the backyard.

When my own sons were five years old, I took them to a workshop for dads and sons at Home Depot. We built things out of wood, and I bought them each their first toolbox. As they were growing up, I added tools to their toolbox, hoping they'd have a full set by the time they left home to live on their own. They've helped me assemble and repair things over the years, so I've been able to teach them how to use different tools for different jobs.

Along the way, I wanted to help them gather tools for being strong and smart as well. I hoped that by the time they left home to live on their own they would have a full set of emotional tools to use when they felt sad or lonely, angry or afraid, hopeless or happy.

My other grandfather loved to fish. He gave me my first tackle box. It's an old, rusty blue lunch box with compartments for bait, hooks, lures, bobbers, sinkers, and swivels. He taught me to use the items inside with patience and precision. He bought me my first pole, and I learned to bait the line, catch and release, watch and wait. I still have that tackle box in my office today. He wrote my name on the front, and although it's faded after many decades, you can still see his handwriting.

A toolbox contains what you need for building. A tackle box contains the supplies you need for fishing. Just as a builder would never show up at a site without his tools, a fisherman would never head to open water without a tackle box.

I think it's equally important to have the tools you need for life. Tools for handling conflict, frustration, transitions, and loss. These are the tools that make you strong and smart. These tools help you build emotional muscles. You need these tools right now as a son, brother, student, athlete, and friend. You'll need these tools in the future as a husband, father, friend, and coworker.

Sadly, many boys and men don't have the tools they need for life. They can't name their feelings, and they don't know what to do with them. They are like hikers lost in the woods. They are like pilots flying in circles, unsure where to land. They are like athletes who don't know the plays of the game.

I want you to feel prepared and practiced. The more we practice with these tools, the stronger the emotional muscles get and the more prepared we are to face whatever comes our way.

Ask your parents if they will help you buy a toolbox or lunch box where you can start to collect strong and smart tools. Start thinking about and writing down things you might like to put inside your Strong and Smart Toolbox like stress balls, fidget spinners, a feelings chart, hand grips, thinking putty, a balloon, a notebook, et cetera. We'll talk more about your toolbox and narrow down what to put in it later in this book.

Brain and Body

Being prepared starts with paying attention. Have you ever been in the car with your mom or dad and a warning light came on the dashboard? Cars are designed to signal us in how to care for them. We get a signal when a tire's air pressure is low, the oil needs changing, or routine maintenance is required. As long as we respond to the signal with adding air to a tire, changing the oil, or topping off the wiper fluid, the car continues running successfully.

If we get a check engine light, it may be a bigger issue. It could just be time for a service appointment, or it might be something more. Our bodies work in the same way. We have internal signals and sirens alerting us to something needing attention.

Your body may signal you when your heart is racing faster than normal. You may feel tightness in your back or shoulders. You may feel a flutter in your stomach or notice it's hard to swallow. You may observe your jaw is tight or your fists are clenched. There are many ways our bodies send us signals.

Our job is to pay attention to those signals and make a plan. If we ignore the signals, they might go away for a little while, but when they come back, things are often a little worse. It's like a volcano that eventually erupts with hot lava and spills out everywhere. Feelings that are ignored and pushed down inside can eventually erupt like a volcano.

Color in the areas of your body that signal you when you have feelings.

The Water Experiment

Ask your mom or dad to help you fill up a pot with water. Make sure the pot is almost full. Stand by the stove and watch what happens when the water starts to boil. Feelings are like the water. The more we put in, the fuller the pot gets. When the water starts to boil, it can spill out all over the stove and make a mess. If someone is standing too close, they may get burned by the hot water. Either way, the water becomes dangerous.

Ask your parents to turn off the stove and pour out half the water. Then turn the stove back on and see what happens. The water will start to boil again, but it takes longer to reach the top because the pot isn't as full. Any time we let feelings out, we keep from getting close to spilling over.

Talking about our feelings is one of the best ways to keep them from spilling out like boiling water. Writing or drawing pictures in a journal can help too. We will talk about other ways to get the feelings out as we go along.

The Balloon Experiment

Try blowing a small amount of air into a balloon. Notice how there's still plenty of room and no chance the balloon will pop. Let the air out slowly (sometimes it makes a funny sound). Air inside the balloon is like feelings in our body. Letting the air out is like sharing those feelings with a friend, family member, counselor, or coach.

This time, blow air into the balloon until you think it might pop. What did it feel like to get close to the point of popping? Did you feel nervous? What would you think about trying to add more air now?

Adding in more air to an already full balloon is a lot like the volcano erupting or the water boiling over. Things feel scary when you get to that point. Holding in feelings is like walking around with a balloon that has too much air, waiting for something bad to happen.

Calming and Coping

What are some other things we can do to help our brains and bodies when we have a lot of feelings inside of us? In addition to talking, drawing, or writing about them, we can also find some calming and coping strategies.

You may have already had some practice doing this. Some classrooms have a "calm corner" where students can go to take a break and calm themselves during the school day. If your teacher doesn't have one, you could tell him or her about it and maybe add one to your classroom.

You can also create one at home. You can name it anything you want. Talk with your mom or dad about a good spot in your house for this. It might be the garage or the playroom. It might be in the corner of the den or the laundry room. It's a good idea to put it somewhere where *anyone* in the family could use it easily. Some boys simply call it the Space, but you could call it one of these names:

The Calm Corner
The Settle Space
The Peace Place
The Coping Cave
The Feelings Fort

Or you could use your family's name. Something like . . .

The Hendersons' Hideout
The Quintins' Quarters
The Petersons' Place

The Fishers' Fort

The Connors' Corner

Brainstorm on some things to put in this space. Maybe some pillows to punch, scream into, or throw safely. Maybe an exercise ball to do the same with. You could add a mini trampoline to jump on or a punching bag or a beanbag to punch. You could add a yoga mat to practice yoga or to do push-ups and sit-ups on. You could include a bucket of art supplies to draw or color. You could add some Silly Putty to squeeze or shape. You could include Bubble Wrap from a package to stomp on or cardboard boxes to tear up and recycle. There are so many options to include. Think about objects that allow you to release some energy.

Movement

As guys, we often have a lot of intensity and energy inside of us when we have big feelings. It's why we accidentally start to yell, hit, kick, scream, or throw things when we have big emotions. Our bodies are sending us a signal that we need to release that energy and intensity. This space is the perfect place to go to get the energy out. Otherwise, we may accidentally throw something that breaks or yell at someone we love. If we start to pay attention to those big feelings and go straight to this "work it through" space, we can keep from making choices that might get us in trouble or hurt our relationships. Moving our bodies is one of the quickest, easiest ways to reset our brains.

Moving our **bodies** is one of the quickest, easiest ways to **reset** our **brains**.

Make a list of movement strategies you could do in the Space, like push-ups, pull-ups, sit-ups, burpees, jumping, leg lifts, yoga, or stretches.

Toolbox or Tackle Box

You remember me talking about the toolbox I had when I was a boy? Or the tackle box I took fishing? You may have already asked your parents for one. You can put supplies in it and keep it in the Space at home and take it with you when you go places. That way, you have tools with you wherever you go.

I know some boys who like to keep their toolbox in the car if they feel nervous on the way to school or in the pickup line. I know some boys who put things in a pencil pouch to have on the bus ride to and from school if they've had a tough day. These items can go with you when you visit grandparents or extended family, go on vacation or take a trip, or head to the doctor's office for a checkup or finger prick. You could call this the Calm Container or Settle Down Storage. You could fill the box or bin with Silly Putty, stress balls, fidget toys, hand weights, balloons, art supplies, or journals. There are so many good ideas. It's just a matter of using these good ideas to help you work through the big emotions.

Now that you know more strategies for working through big emotions, take some time to write down on the next page what you want to put in your container (look back at your notes on page 15 for inspiration), and ask your parents to help you buy the container and the things on your list.

Feelings Chart

There are two other great items to put in the Calm Corner or the Calm Container. One is a feelings chart. You can find one online at raisingboysandgirls.com. It's a great tool to have when you're trying to figure out the different feelings you're having inside of you.

Spend a few minutes talking about the different feelings with your parent to make sure you know what they are.

Top Five List

The second item for your toolbox (or tackle box) is a Top Five List. This is a list of coping skills. Coping is learning to manage emotions in a healthy way. Include on your list some of the movement strategies you came up with for the Space. You've already done some great brainstorming for your Top Five List. But leave room for one more great idea. It's called **combat breathing**. Many years ago, I did some work with Navy SEALs and Army Rangers. These are highly skilled and trained soldiers who are assigned special missions. They are superheroes themselves. They have to make difficult and important decisions in complicated circumstances. And they have to be able to settle their brains and bodies to make those decisions in a split second. Combat breathing is the quickest way to settle the brain and body.

Think about the word *combat*. *Combat* means "to fight or contend against." We are fighting or contending against the tendency to yell, hit, kick, scream, or hurt someone. The Bible verse Ephesians 4:26 tells us, "In your anger do not sin." That important verse is reminding us of two things. First, it's reminding us that we are going to feel anger sometimes, and that's okay. Anger isn't a bad feeling. It's just a feeling. Sometimes anger is the feeling and the fuel we need to help us fight against the bad things in this world.

Second, the verse is reminding us, when we feel anger, not to sin— not to hurt ourselves or others. Some people become really hurtful when they feel anger. They aren't fighting for the right things; they are fighting against the wrong things. Remember, sometimes hurt people *hurt* people.

For example, have you ever felt angry and your mom tried to help you calm down? Instead of letting her help you breathe and calm your brain and body, maybe you yelled at her or threw something across the room. That's fighting against the wrong things. In that example, you used anger to hurt someone you love instead of learning to fight the good fight.

Combat Breathing

Back to breathing, let's practice some combat breathing to make sure you know how it's done. Start by tracing the shape of a square on your leg. This will help you learn to breathe in and out at a good pace. On the first line of the square, breathe in and then pause in the corner. On the second line of the square, breathe out slowly and pause again in the corner. On the third line, breathe in and pause in the corner, and on the fourth line breathe out. As you are tracing the shape of the square, you now realize your finger is back where it started. Be sure to breathe in through your nose, out through your mouth, and down to your belly. Try again and count to four in your head as you trace each line. Those are good numbers to help you make sure you aren't breathing too fast to get the good calming effect.

Practice combat breathing often to make sure you get really good at doing it. You can practice in the car, in bed at night, before school in the morning, or even during a basketball game.

Many boys I work with do this before a spelling test at school under their desk, where no one even knows it's happening. One boy I meet with does it at the free throw line before the referee hands him the ball in a basketball game. He puts his hands on his legs, and no one can even tell he's doing it. It helps him calm his brain and body before he makes the shot. You can do this anytime and anywhere. Before a race, a timed test, a finger prick at the doctor, a penalty kick in soccer, batting in baseball, or a presentation in class.

> Practice combat **breathing** often to make sure you get **really** good at it.

27

I wear a watch that tracks my heart rate. What would you guess happens to my heart rate when I practice combat breathing? Do you think my heart rate goes up or goes down? If you guessed down, you're right. Anytime we practice combat breathing, it slows down our heart rate. It also redistributes the blood flow to different parts of the brain and body.

When we are emotionally charged, our pupils dilate so we can see danger more clearly. Blood flow shifts to the large muscles so we are tensed and ready. Even our stomach jumps on board by decreasing digestive activity, so we have extra energy to fight or run away. This is a great state to be in if we encounter a scary animal or person and we need to run away. God made our bodies so we could run faster and fight harder in case of danger. But sometimes we feel worried about a spelling test or sharing at circle time, and this is not a good state to be in, so we have to calm our brains and bodies.

Practice four rounds of combat breathing with your parent. Pay attention to how your body feels before and after.

Understanding the Brain

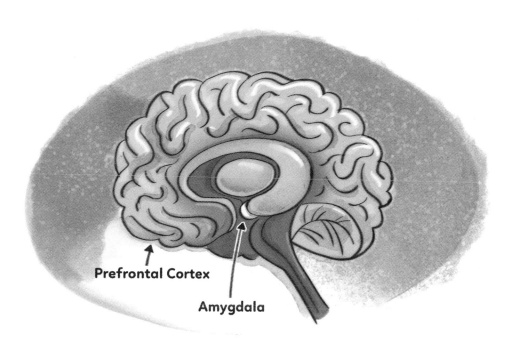

Prefrontal Cortex

Amygdala

When my dog, Owen, is at home, he likes to take a nap on the front porch. Sometimes a friend stops by and Owen starts barking at them before he realizes it's someone friendly he knows. He also does this when our neighborhood postman brings the mail. These people aren't here to hurt us, they are here to help us. Once he realizes that, he stops barking and starts wagging his tail.

Our brains are a lot like that. Sometimes they sense danger when it's not real. We get worked up rather than staying calm, cool, and collected. It's like when a fire alarm goes off accidentally. There's not a real fire, but we start to panic anyway.

Let's talk about two important parts of the brain. The front part of the brain is the prefrontal cortex, which houses our frontal lobes. Many people call this part of the brain the "wise owl." The wise owl helps us

1. think rationally and
2. manage emotions.

The back part of the brain houses the amygdala. Many people call this part of the brain the "barking dog." The barking dog helps us

1. notice danger and
2. react.

We need the dog to bark when there is true danger. If a burglar was trying to break into the house, that would be the perfect time for Owen to bark. But not if the mailman is trying to deliver the mail, or if a friend is stopping by for a visit.

When the dog barks, the owl flies away.

When the wise owl flies away, we have trouble thinking rationally and managing our emotions. We have to quiet the barking dog so the wise owl can return.

Calming and coping strategies help quiet the barking dog so the wise owl can return. Any time we practice combat breathing or head to the Calm Corner, we are helping quiet the barking dog. Any time we go to our Space to try out our Top Five List, we help the barking dog stop so the wise owl can help us think rationally and manage our emotions.[1]

Another way to understand the brain is with our hand. Dr. Dan Siegel and Dr. Tina Payne Bryson created the hand model to explain these parts of the brain. Hold up your hand and all five fingers. The thumb represents the barking dog, and the four fingers represent the wise owl. When we quiet the barking dog, we tuck our thumb into the palm of our hand and pull the four fingers over top to make a

1. "Thinking Brain: The Wise Owl," *The Behavior Hub*, September 17, 2020, https://www .thebehaviorhub.com/blog/2020/9/17/emotional-brain-prefrontal-cortex-wise-owl.

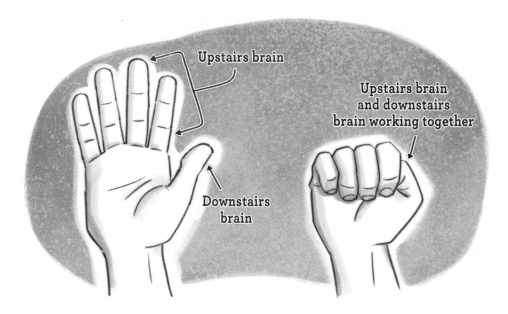

Upstairs brain

Upstairs brain and downstairs brain working together

Downstairs brain

fist. The closed fist looks like the shape of the brain. The four fingers represent the prefrontal cortex, or what Dr. Siegel and Dr. Bryson call the upstairs brain. The thumb represents the limbic system, where the amygdala is housed. They call this the downstairs brain.

When the amygdala gets triggered, or the dog starts barking, we flip our lid. The fingers open up and the thumb comes out. When the fingers come up, the wise owl flies away. When we flip our lid, we stop thinking rationally and we can't manage our emotions. When we flip our lid, the downstairs brain is in charge and we need the upstairs brain to help. We need our upstairs brain and our downstairs brain to work *together*, not *separately*.

Think about the upstairs brain as the thinking part of the brain. The downstairs brain is the emotional part of the brain. The goal is to always involve the upstairs and the downstairs parts of the brain. We want to always include thinking *and* feeling.

I know some grown-ups who have a hard time involving thinking. They are always making emotional decisions without thinking it through. I also know some grown-ups who only involve thinking. They forget the importance of considering how people will feel about the decisions they've made. *Integration* is a big word that simply means we are including thinking *and* feeling. We are involving the upstairs *and* downstairs parts of the brain.[2]

2. Daniel J. Siegel and Tina Payne Bryson, *The Whole-Brain Child: 12 Revolutionary Strategies to Nurture Your Child's Developing Mind* (New York: Bantam Books, 2011), 59, 62–63.

That's why having the Top Five List is so helpful. Even if we can't remember our practices, we can take a look at the list we made when the wise owl was around and start practicing those things to make the barking dog stop.

Understanding this is so important. You can tell your parents the wise owl flew away, and you need to go to the Calm Corner to make the barking dog stop barking.

Your mom and dad could help you out by saying things like

"The dog is barking," or

"I think we've flipped our lids," or

"The downstairs brain is in charge"

to help you remember what to do next. You could even use a visual cue like the stop sign with your hand—holding out all the fingers and thumb—to show you've flipped your lid and need to stop talking it through and work it through instead. One of the biggest mistakes we make is trying to talk it through before working it through.

We need our **upstairs** brain and our **downstairs** brain to work *together*.

Work it through, THEN talk it through.

Quiet the barking dog, THEN the wise owl returns.

Practice the hand model. Show your parents what the hand looks like when the dog is barking and the owl flies away. Show them what it looks like when the upstairs and downstairs brains are working together.

Hopefully by now you've done some brainstorming with your parents about creating a space in your house where anyone in the family can go when they need to work through some big feelings so they don't accidentally try to work them through on a person.

As you create your Top Five List, don't forget to add combat breathing and some movement strategies. Breathing and movement are two of the quickest ways to reset the brain and body. If you start to notice that some of the ideas on your Top Five List aren't helping as much, you can always scratch those off and replace them with new ideas. If you notice the Space you created isn't in a good spot, you can always move it to a new location. Having a resilient mindset means that if something isn't working, we don't keep trying the same thing over and over. We try something new.

Here's another important reminder as you are working on ideas for your Top Five List: Don't use ideas that involve a screen. Screens are an escape, not a strategy. I know how much fun screens can be, and it's okay to have some screen time with healthy limits that your parents set. Keep using screens for fun, but not for strategies. We don't want to train our brains to use screens for calming down. First of all, screens make our brains more active, not more settled. The strategies we are working with are ones that have more of a calming effect and involve effort of some kind. Staring at a screen doesn't involve effort of any kind.

> Screens make our brains more **active**, not more **settled**.

I'd also remind you that practice makes progress. Sometimes people say that practice makes perfect, but I don't think that's true. There are plenty of things I've practiced in my life that I didn't do perfectly. But in everything I've ever practiced, I could see progress. Practice combat breathing and movement strategies the same way you practice riding your bike, shooting hoops, or learning a new instrument or sight words. We have to practice at new things to get better at them.

In order to become emotionally strong, we have to practice these:

Breathing and movement
Space and strategies

We have to practice going to our Space instead of flipping our lid. We have to practice quieting the barking dog so the wise owl won't fly away.

Walk It Off

Have you ever watched sports on TV or been to a live game and seen players walking up and down the court or field? Sometimes coaches or teammates will even challenge a player by saying, "Walk it off." I remember the first time I heard my basketball coach invite me to do that. It was during a game, and an opponent had fouled me in a cheap way. I felt angry when it happened. I was glad the referee saw it and called the foul, but it felt wrong. The player even smirked when he looked back at me, like he was glad he did it anyway.

I took my coach's advice and walked from side to side while the referee was announcing the foul and preparing to hand me the ball. It felt helpful to move around instead of standing still. That movement was resetting my brain and helping me quiet the barking dog inside of me.

Movement is always helpful for **resetting** the brain and body.

I want the upstairs brain on board when I make a free throw. The upstairs brain helps me calculate how hard and far to throw the ball when I make the shot. If only the downstairs brain was in the mix, I'd be more likely to throw too far or too hard. All that anger inside of me could cause me to slam the ball against the goal but not hit the net.

I've seen players walk it off at Wimbledon, the NFL, the MLB, the NBA, the NHL, and about every other professional sports organization. I've been watching the Summer Olympics, and I have witnessed gymnasts, swimmers, runners, and lots of other athletes do it as well.

It's a reminder that movement is always helpful for resetting the brain and body. Think of it this way: Move it or lose it. That's one of the reasons going to the Space is so helpful. We start the "walk it off" process when we move from where we are standing to the Calm Corner. We keep the "walk it off" process going when we do some push-ups, pull-ups, sit-ups, jumping, squeezing, screaming, or whatever else helps us work it through.

Once we release the energy and intensity, we can do some breathing, and then we are ready for some thinking.

Moving → Breathing → Thinking → Talking

Once our upstairs brain jumps on board, we get to the thinking and talking. We can check the feelings chart to figure out what different emotions we were experiencing, and we can also give our emotions a number.

Perspective Scale

If you've ever been to the ER for an injury, you might have been asked to rate your pain. "On a scale of one to ten, what's your pain?" We need to know the difference between level-two pain and level-nine pain. If we can't accurately gauge the pain, the doctor can't accurately treat the pain.

The same is true for all the events in life. We need to know the difference between a two event in life and a nine event in life. For example, for me, losing my car keys is a one and losing a family member is a ten. If I react to small things in life in a big way, it's difficult for my friends and family to know how to best support me.

Just like I need to be able to tell someone exactly what I'm feeling, I need to be able to tell them how big of an event it is. If I lose my car keys, I want to be able to say, "I feel worried, and I need help finding them." I don't want to say, "I'M THE WORST PERSON IN THE WORLD!" over losing my car keys. First of all, it's not true. Second of all, it's not helpful.

Many people use big words and scary statements to talk about their feelings and events because they don't have an emotional vocabulary. They can't accurately name their feelings and rate their experience.

I'd like you to spend some time talking with your parents about your **perspective scale**. On the previous page, list what your one-to-ten events would be. While you are working on the list, you may decide to move some answers around, and that's okay.

When you have a difficult day, after you've done some moving and breathing, then talk with your parents about what you were feeling and what number you think the event was based on your scale.

Detective Work

When I was a kid, I loved to read books. I found a series called
THE HARDY BOYS about two brothers who are detectives and solve
mysteries. I think I read more than fifty books in this series, and I
would dream about becoming a detective myself. I like to think that
in some ways I did become a detective. I help boys and their families
find clues. I help them make discoveries and solve mysteries. Just not
quite in the way I imagined it when I was seven years old.

Using the perspective scale takes some detective work. Figuring out
the difference between a five event and a seven event requires some
clues and clever thinking. You have to be strong and smart to do that.

Identifying exactly what I'm feeling requires some detective work
as well. Somewhere around age nine or ten, boys start channeling
all primary emotions into anger. What does that mean?

It means that anger is on top, but there's always something underneath. Anger is what most often comes out, but there's always

another feeling below it. Once we've done some movement and breathing, we can do some **thinking and talking**. When we get the upstairs brain on board, we're ready to do some good detective work.

Think about it like the Incredible Hulk and his alter-ego, Dr. Banner. The Hulk is like the downstairs brain and Dr. Banner is like the upstairs brain. The Hulk wouldn't make a great detective, but Dr. Banner certainly would.

We need the detective work to figure out what's underneath the anger. For example, I recently talked with a boy who'd just started first grade. His teacher asked each student to make a poster and put five photos on the poster. Each photo had to tell his new classmates something about him. He and his mom looked at over twenty photos of their family, his dog, a birthday party, a soccer team, grandparents, a favorite vacation spot, a Disney trip, his new bike, his scout troop, and countless others. Not only was it difficult to narrow it down to five photos, but he had trouble getting down to ten. They talked through all the options, and he was finding it harder and harder to make a decision.

His mom noticed that he was starting to yell when she made suggestions, so she encouraged him to go to the Feelings Fort to jump on the mini trampoline and squeeze some stress balls. (He liked to do both at the same time.) He told her he didn't need to go and kept looking at the pictures. His wise mom could tell that he was flipping his lid and his upstairs brain was offline. Dr. Banner had left the building and the Hulk was emerging.

She challenged him to go to the Feelings Fort again when she noticed his jaw and fists were clenched tightly. At that moment, he slammed his fist on the table and yelled, "I'M NOT ANGRY!"

At that exact moment, his dad walked into the room and heard him yelling. He told him the dog was barking loudly and the wise owl had flown away. He asked him to go with him to the Feelings Fort, and they went together. They did some jumping, yelling, and even crying. Then they did some breathing. Through tears, the boy told his parents he was worried people would make fun of him when he shared the photos and stories.

That's good detective work. He was able to figure out that underneath the anger was worry. That's often the case. But the Incredible Hulk couldn't figure that out on his own.

We need our upstairs brain to do the detective work. We need the detective work to find out what's underneath the anger.

He needed the Feelings Fort to work through the big emotions. He needed movement and breathing to get to the thinking and talking. He needed to work it through so he could talk it through.

If he hadn't listened to his parents encouraging him, he'd have gotten stuck in the anger. If he'd never gone to the Feelings Fort, he'd have struggled to finish the project.

The Work of Sleep

Speaking of worry, a lot of kids have trouble with worry and fear at night. Turning off your thoughts and falling asleep can be tough. The work of sleep is just that—WORK! It takes work to settle the mind and body at night. Anytime worry, fear, or anxiety is in the mix, our mind starts moving backward or forward. Anxiety resides in the past or the future. We are worrying about something that has already happened (and might happen again), or something that could happen in the future. Our job becomes jumping out of the past or future and landing in the *present*. If you notice that worry or fear creeps in around bedtime, here are some helpful strategies that could make the work of sleep easier and more successful.

Progressive muscle relaxation (PMR) is one I teach boys all the time. You can do this side by side with one of your parents and take turns calling out parts of the body to tense and relax. Start at the top of your body and work your way down. Tense your forehead and then relax your forehead. Squeeze your eyes shut and then relax them. Move to your nose, mouth, neck, shoulders, chest, stomach, hips, thighs, knees, calves, and feet. Once you finish, you can start at the bottom of your body and work your way back to the top. Give yourself plenty of time to relax and breathe after the tensing and tightening.

Gratitude is a proven way to reset the brain. Make yourself think of five things from the day that you're grateful for. Maybe one of those things was waffles for breakfast, a bike ride, playing a board game with your family, meeting a new friend at school, or playing kickball at recess. Think through all the events and people throughout your day and see how long a list you can develop as you move your mind away from worry and toward gratitude.

The Counting Game is another great way to move your mind away from worry and engage in some productive work. Pick a number as your starting point. Let's say twenty-five. Then count backward by fives. Depending on how good you are at math, you can pick a higher number as your starting point and a harder number for counting backward. For example, you could start with one hundred and count backward by sevens. You can also count forward if you like that better.

It takes **practice** to get **good** at these **sleep** strategies.

The Color Game can be done in the light or the dark. Pick any color and identify everything in your room that has that color in it. If you know your room really well, you could do it in the dark, calling out the objects without seeing them.

5-4-3-2-1 works with the five senses: hearing, taste, smell, touch, and sight. You can go in any order you'd like. Start by listing five things you hear, then four things you taste, three things you smell, two things you touch, and one thing you see.

Three Doors involves thinking about three of your favorite places. Maybe your grandparents' house, a favorite vacation spot, or Disney World. Imagine in your mind walking through the door of one of those favorite spots. Describe what you see, what smells you notice, what sounds you hear, and any other senses. Maybe you can taste your favorite meal at that spot. Maybe you can touch something there in your mind like sand on the beach or warm water from the ocean. Walk through the doors of all three places, allowing time for your senses to remember.

It takes practice to get good at these. You can do them with your parent in the beginning and then eventually by yourself. They are great to use if you have trouble falling asleep when you're away from home at camp or a sleepover. You need to practice these the same way you practice spelling words, a sport you love, or riding your bike. It takes time and it's easy to give up when the worry starts to sneak back in, but keep practicing until you get really good at them. They can also be used in the daytime. Try the Counting Game, Color Game, or 5-4-3-2-1 next time you are at the doctor's office before a checkup or at the dentist's office to have your teeth cleaned.

Scripture and Statements

You may have a favorite verse you love as well. Write that verse down in the space below. Use that verse as a reminder and a regulation strategy (I'll explain what *regulation* means more in the next section). Sometimes our brains get stuck on a certain thought. Maybe it's a worry or a frustration. Memorizing Scripture and speaking it out loud to yourself is a great way to interrupt those "stuck" thoughts and to hide God's Word in your heart.

You could do the same thing with a favorite quote or line from a movie. I know a boy who used to say, "Just keep swimming" from *Finding Nemo* when he felt overwhelmed. Another boy would say, "No one is perfect—that's why pencils have erasers" when he felt frustrated with himself while doing homework. Another boy memorized 1 Peter 5:7: "Cast all your anxiety on him because he cares for you."

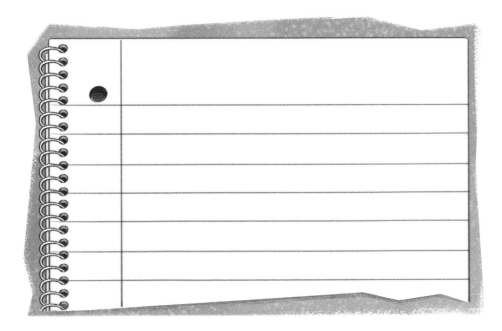

Integration and Regulation

I want to teach you some big words. These are important words. The words are *integration* and *regulation*. *Integration* is uniting different things. It's incorporating thinking and feeling. Integration is when our upstairs and downstairs brains are working together. Using the hand model for yourself and letting your parents use it as a visual cue are great ways to get more integrated.

Regulation is managing our emotions. It's some of the most important work we do. Regulation lets us be more in control of our emotions than our emotions are in control of us. Regulation is what keeps us from turning into the Incredible Hulk every day.

Integration and regulation are what make us able to use our Spidey sense. These skills help us do the important detective work of figuring out what's underneath the anger.

Integration and regulation help us be more of who we want to be in the world. We can be more heroic and less hurtful. Regulation and integration allow us to be strong and smart.

Help and Hope

When we practice integration and regulation, we not only help ourselves but we position ourselves to help others. It's what allows Superman, Spider-Man, and Batman to notice the people around them who need help. We can see our friends and family differently when we are in an integrated and regulated state.

Recently I was at an airport, and my flight was delayed. I started to feel tension in my neck and shoulders. One man started to yell at the gate agent, who had absolutely no control over whether the plane departed on time. The man flipped his lid, and his downstairs brain was doing all the talking. He banged his fist on the counter and shouted.

As I paid attention to the signs and signals in my body, I decided to do some regulation work in the airport. First, I took a walk from one end of the terminal to the other. Second, I found a quiet spot and did some stretching. Third, I decided to do some combat breathing. Fourth, I walked to the gift shop and bought a bottle of cold water. It's just always a good idea to hydrate, isn't it?

What I noticed next was that my heart rate slowed down. I could see it happening on my Apple Watch. I noticed the tension in my neck and shoulders was starting to go away. The flight was still delayed, but I felt more settled in my brain and body.

I also started to notice people around me who needed help. There was an older passenger who was struggling to find the newly scheduled arrival time so they could alert their family members. I helped this passenger look online on my phone and then make the call.

I noticed a little boy who was getting restless. We played a game together, and it was good for both our brains to think about something besides the waiting.

I noticed another passenger with a service dog who was getting thirsty. I offered the rest of my water bottle to this passenger, and they poured it in the dog's bowl.

I didn't notice any of these needs before I practiced my skills. If we don't do the work of integration and regulation, we can't see the needs around us. When we do this important work, we become more helpful and supportive to the people in our world.

We can help our parents, siblings, friends, teammates, teachers, and classmates. One of my favorite verses is Micah 6:8, which asks, "And what does the Lord require of you? To act justly and to love mercy and to walk humbly with your God."

Some translations of the Bible talk about doing what is right and being loyal and compassionate. We are capable of being more loving, loyal, merciful, and compassionate when we can see the needs around us. We can do what's right when we settle our brains and bodies, which is the work of regulation and integration.

The world could use more people who are doing what is right and being loyal and compassionate. Developing these important emotional muscles makes us strong and smart. The world needs more strong and smart boys in it. Boys who are committed to acting justly, loving mercy, and walking humbly with God. I'm thankful you'd spend time with this workbook to find out how to get emotionally strong and smart so you can offer those things to the world.

About the Author

David Thomas, LMSW, is the director of family counseling at Daystar Counseling (daystarcounseling.com) in Nashville and the author or coauthor of ten books, including the bestselling *Wild Things: The Art of Nurturing Boys* and *Are My Kids on Track? The 12 Emotional, Social, and Spiritual Milestones Your Child Needs to Reach*. He is a frequent guest on national television shows and podcasts, and he cohosts his own podcast called *Raising Boys and Girls*; he has been featured in publications like the *Washington Post* and *USA Today*; and he speaks across the country.

He and his wife, Connie, have a daughter, twin sons, and a yellow lab named Owen. You can follow David on social media @raising boysandgirls and find the latest parenting resources at raisingboys andgirls.com.